RACHEL GOENKA'S
Adventures
with Mithai

RACHEL GOENKA'S

Adventures
with Mithai

INDIAN SWEETS GET A MODERN MAKEOVER

HarperCollins *Publishers* India

For my son, Kabir.

May you always have sweetness in your life.

INTRODUCTION

DESSERTS

CHEESECAKES & CAKES

TRUFFLES*

* Eggless

MACARONS

ICE CREAMS, KULFIS & SORBETS

Contents

Why mithai?

I'M ASKED THIS QUESTION every time I share the concept of this book with anyone.

It baffles people, especially since my culinary training is in French patisserie. I am known for desserts like my Red Velvet Cake, Salted Caramel and Chocolate Mousse Profiteroles, Sticky Toffee Pudding, and Basil and Dark Chocolate Fondant. Which is why making mithai the focus of my first cookbook came as a big surprise to everyone.

I have always loved mithai. Some of my favourites are kaju katli (I can eat an entire box in a single sitting) and boondi laddoos. Motichoor laddoos are another favourite but I love the sugary boondi version better.

My biggest weakness though, has always been Mysore pak. Every time anyone – anyone (my father's friend's sister's uncle even) – visits Chennai, a box must be brought back for me from Sri Krishna Sweets. My dad is diabetic, and this is the only indulgence we share, cheating together – he on the betterment of his blood sugar and I on my waist line. I love how the ghee-saturated goodie melts in my mouth.

So you see. My love affair with mithai has existed for a long time.

I have always loved experimenting with food. Having studied classic French patisserie at Le Cordon Bleu in London and then trained under celebrity Irish chef Rachel Allen, I have a deep appreciation for classic and traditional techniques. But the joy of the culinary arts is to add your own twist to it!

That approach was what gave me the confidence to open my first restaurant, The Sassy Spoon, at the age of 24. Even then I knew I did not want to do conventional, run-on-the-mill flavours and techniques. And so 'Sassy' became synonymous with unconventional, brazen, out-of-the-box and cheeky, which is what my food and desserts are. I dared to pair balsamic vinegar with chocolate, goat's cheese with sugar, coffee with cream cheese.

It wasn't until the first Diwali rolled around, that I decided I wanted to apply the same sassiness to traditional Indian desserts as well. After all, it was an eclectic European restaurant and if I had to serve Indian desserts then they had to be done in a contemporary way.

That's when this mithai craze of mine really took off. I would sit for hours and just taste different types of mithais, and make notes on what flavour combinations I thought would work and then experiment. I also loved combining different Indian flavours. One of my proudest moments was a sweet khandvi, a thin layer of sweet saffron pasta with pistachio cream and rabri. To represent the mustard seeds on top I used balsamic caviar. I did another dessert called 7 Textures of Mithai (a play on one of my classics – 7 Textures of Hazelnut and Chocolate). That was a combination of khoya barfi, masala chai ganache, Mahim halwa, pista sponge, saffron mousse, white chocolate disks and cardamom basundi sauce.

Every Diwali I experimented with traditional flavours and I loved doing it so much that I started developing different confections for different festivals. Indian-flavoured Chocolate Modaks are always a hit during Ganpati!

Rachel Goenka's Adventures with Mithai is the product of seven years of experimentation, toil and quirk. The inspiration behind these recipes is simple – elevating mithai in a fun way by taking our favourites and jazzing them up! All the mithais used in this book are either store-bought or easily made at home. A lot of the ingredients are probably already lying in your pantry.

Mithai is amazing on its own, but there is so much more that you can do with it. It's extremely versatile and these recipes will show you just how much. I have used classic techniques and familiar ingredients, but the flavour combinations are far from ordinary.

In these 50 recipes you will find a way to take your favourite mithai and add a contemporary twist to it by transforming it into cheesecakes, truffles, macrons or ice creams. Whether you are entertaining at home on a festive occasion, or want an unconventional yet traditional dessert table or even just want to introduce mithai to others in a more familiar way, these recipes have you covered.

Welcome to the adventure. I promise it will be sweet.

De

sserts

Lemongrass Panna Cotta with Vermicelli Kheer

The citrusy, slightly gingery flavour of lemongrass adds a gentle scent to this elegant and light milk-based dessert.

SERVES 6

INGREDIENTS

KHEER
Ghee 15 g
Pistachios 15 g
Cashew nuts 15 g
Cardamom 3
Rice vermicelli
(seviyan), roasted 50 g
Milk 250 ml
Castor sugar 15 g
Condensed milk 20 g

PANNA COTTA
Lemongrass 2 stalks,
chopped
Milk 375 ml
Heavy cream 125 g
Castor sugar 75 g
Gelatin 1 tsp
50 ml warm water

GARNISH
Vermicelli, deep-fried,
30 g
Pistachios, blanched
30 g

✳ For the panna cotta, lightly crush the lemongrass with the back of a spoon. Add it to the 375 ml milk, heat and reduce for 5 minutes on a low flame. Cover and refrigerate overnight so the flavour steeps through the milk.

✳ To make the kheer, heat ghee in a pan and sauté the pistachios and cashew nuts until golden brown. Crush the cardamom pods, add to the pan and sauté further. Add the roasted vermicelli and stir.

✳ Pour in 250 ml milk and heat till the vermicelli is cooked. Add 15 g sugar and condensed milk, stir and set aside.

✳ Soak the gelatin in warm water.

✳ Heat the cream and 75 g sugar, then strain the lemongrass-flavoured milk (made the night before) into the cream. Heat until the sugar melts, then add the soaked gelatin.

✳ Pour half cup of the panna cotta liquid into a martini glass and refrigerate for an hour.

✳ Layer the kheer over the chilled panna cotta and let it set in the refrigerator before serving.

✳ Garnish with vermicelli and pistachios.

If you love the seviyan kheer made at home, you can use your family recipe instead of mine.

Rasmalai & Saffron Mousse with Pistachio Sponge

This versatile dessert spells Diwali for me! It's a great choice for your dining table during the festive season, because who doesn't love rasmalai?

SERVES 6

INGREDIENTS

PISTACHIO SPONGE
Icing sugar 60 g
Flour 23 g
Pistachio, powdered 90 g
Egg whites 3
Castor sugar 45 g

SAFFRON MOUSSE
Milk 62 ml
A generous pinch of saffron
Whipping cream 200 g
Gelatin 3/4 tsp
Warm water 50 ml
Egg yolks 2
Castor sugar 75 g
White chocolate pieces 50 g
Kesar rasmalai 12 pieces

GARNISH
Sutarfeni

* Preheat the oven to 180°C and line a 9x5-inch baking tray with butter paper.

* To make the pistachio sponge, sieve the icing sugar, flour and pistachio powder together.

* Make a meringue by whisking the egg whites until stiff. Add the castor sugar and keep whisking till you get stiff peaks.

* Fold the pistachio mixture into the meringue.

* Pour the sponge mix into the tray and spread evenly.

* Bake the sponge until it is firm, for about 18 to 20 minutes. Set aside to cool.

* To make the mousse, heat the milk, add the saffron and allow it to steep. Cover and set aside for 30 minutes.

* In a bowl, whisk the whipping cream till it holds soft peaks. Refrigerate.

* Soak the gelatin in warm water.

* Whisk the egg yolks and the sugar over a double boiler, until light and foamy.

* Add the saffron-flavoured milk and mix well, then add the white chocolate pieces.

* Warm the mix slightly over the double boiler to melt the chocolate. Add the soaked gelatin and mix thoroughly.

* Add one tablespoon of whipped cream to the saffron mixture to cool it down and then fold in the remaining.

* To assemble the dessert, cut the pistachio sponge into circles that will fit inside a serving glass (use a cutter to make even circles).

* Layer the dessert by placing a slice of pistachio sponge in the glass. Top the sponge with an even layer of saffron mousse, followed by a piece of rasmalai. Set in the refrigerator for 15 minutes and then repeat the layering process.

* Serve chilled and garnish with sutarfeni before serving.

This dish works nicely as a cake as well. Simply bake the sponge in a round cake tin and then layer the dessert in a ring mould lined with acetate paper. Chill and unmould.

Mohan Bhog Crème Éclairs

There are many variations of fluffy choux pastry; these éclairs have a crunchy sablé crust. The light creamy filling, flavoured with Mohan Bhog from Sweet Bengal, gives this dessert a unique texture.

SERVES 15

INGREDIENTS
CHOUX PASTRY
Flour 300 g
Salt 1/2 tbsp
Water 250 ml
Milk 250 ml
Butter 200 g
Eggs 7
Vanilla essence 5 ml

SABLÉ BISCUIT
Butter 150 g
Castor sugar 130 g
Flour 180 g
A few drops of red food colouring gel

FILLING
Mohan bhog from Sweet Bengal 900 g
Heavy cream 220 g

GARNISH
Fresh raspberries and blueberries

✳ Preheat the oven to 200°C.

✳ To make the choux pastry dough, combine 200 g butter, milk and water in a medium-sized saucepan. Bring to a boil, stirring until the butter melts completely. Reduce heat to low, and add 300 g flour and salt.

✳ Stir vigorously until mixture leaves the sides of the pan and begins to form a stiff ball. Remove from heat.

✳ Add the vanilla and the eggs, one at a time, beating well to incorporate completely after each addition. The dough should be of a dropping consistency.

✳ Transfer the dough into a piping bag fitted with a star nozzle and set aside.

✳ Combine all the ingredients for the sablé biscuits and, using a paddle attachment, mix together. The mixture should be deep red in colour.

✳ Roll the biscuit dough into a thin layer (2-mm) and cut 1 1/2-inch strips.

✳ On a baking tray lined with a silicon mat, pipe 4-inch éclairs and top with the sablé strips.

✳ Bake the eclairs for 15 minutes in the preheated oven, then reduce the temperature to 160°C and bake until golden brown, for approximately 20 minutes. Remove the shells from oven and cool on a wire rack.

* Spoon the top cream layer of the Mohan Bhog into a bowl. Add heavy cream and mix together. The reddish centre of the Mohan Bhog will naturally tint the cream a lovely pink. Transfer the cream into a piping bag fitted with a star nozzle.

* Slice the éclairs horizontally and pipe swirls of the cream. Garnish with fresh raspberries and blueberries.

Once you've mastered the éclair, you can make profiteroles by piping the choux pastry into small round balls. Any of the cream-based recipes in this book, like the different types of ganaches from the truffle section (See pp. 80-95), can be used as fillings.

Motichoor Laddoo with Cardamom Mousse

The savoury biscuit base of this jar dessert cuts through the intense sweetness of the laddoos to create a perfect flavour and textural balance.

SERVES 4

INGREDIENTS

PUDDING

Salted biscuits, powdered (I use Monaco) 100 g
Unsalted butter, softened 25 g
Heavy cream 200 ml
Egg yolks 2
Castor sugar 5 tbsp
Gelatin 1/2 tsp
Water, warm 14 ml
Cardamom powder 1/2 tsp
Motichoor laddoos 4 pieces

GARNISH

Almond flakes 2 tbsp

- Mix the powdered biscuits and butter and divide equally in the 4 jars. Press down lightly to form the base of the mousse and chill for an hour or until it sets.
- Whip the cream to soft peaks and refrigerate.
- Soak the gelatin in warm water.
- Whisk the egg yolks and sugar over a double boiler until light and foamy.
- Add the gelatin liquid to the egg yolk and sugar mixture and whisk. Add the cardamom powder.
- Fold the whipped cream into the egg yolks, gently, to make a cardamom mousse.
- Pour 1/3 cup of the mousse over the biscuit base in the chilled jars. Chill for 30 minutes.
- Crush the motichoor laddoos and layer it over the mousse. Garnish with almond flakes and serve chilled.

You can add layer upon layer of motichoor laddoo and cardamom mousse to double the dessert. These tiny jars are great party giveaways and can be personalized with handwritten tags.

Anjeer Barfi Treacle Tart

This classic English treat gets a makeover with the addition of figs three ways – fresh, dried and rich chewy barfi. Get ready to fig in!

SERVES 8

INGREDIENTS

TART BASE
Flour 120 g
Unsalted butter, chilled 60 g
Icing sugar 30 g
Cold water 10 ml
Salt 1/4 tsp

TREACLE FILLING
Golden syrup 300 g
Zest and juice of 1 lemon
White breadcrumbs 30 g
Heavy cream 30 g
Anjeer barfi 200 g
Eggs 4
Dried figs 80 g

GARNISH
Whipped cream 50 g
Fresh figs 2
Fresh blueberries 50 g

❋ Preheat the oven to 170°C.

❋ For the tart base, sift the flour, icing sugar and salt together.

❋ Chop the chilled butter into smaller cubes and gently rub the dry ingredients into the butter, creating a breadcrumb-like texture. Add a few spoons of water at a time and mix with your hands, until the mixture starts to form clumps (only add more water if it looks too dry).

❋ Turn the dough out onto a lightly floured surface. Knead briefly till smooth and flatten into a disc. Wrap with cling film and chill for an hour.

❋ While the dough is chilling, soak the dried figs in warm water for 30 minutes. Chop into eight pieces and set them aside to be used later.

❋ Using a rolling pin, roll the dough into a 9-inch circle and transfer to a 7-inch fluted tart pan with a removable bottom. Trim the excess dough, and chill for 30 minutes.

❋ To blind bake, prick the bottom with a fork and cover with a sheet of parchment paper. Fill with dried beans and bake until the base is set, about 15 minutes.

* Remove the parchment paper and beans and bake until the base is light brown, about 10 minutes.

* While the tart shell is baking, make the filling. In a medium-sized saucepan, heat the golden syrup till it becomes runny.

* Remove from heat and stir in the cream, salt, breadcrumbs, anjeer barfi and lemon zest. Once the mixture has cooled, beat the eggs and add, followed by the chopped figs.

* Pour the filling into the tart shell and bake for 25 to 30 minutes.

* Unmould the tart and cool. Garnish with whipped cream, fresh figs and blueberries.

If you want to intensify the flavour of the figs, you can also add roasted figs either in the filling or as a garnish. If you're using fresh figs as garnish, bake a few pieces, then slice them and drizzle a little honey over the pieces. After cooling, layer them over the fresh figs.

Royal Falooda Trifle

My desi take on an English trifle, this dessert packs in all the flavours of a royal falooda, and the layers make for a gorgeous showstopper of a dessert.

SERVES 20

INGREDIENTS

VANILLA SPONGE
Refined flour 220 g
Baking soda 2 g
Baking powder 1/2 tsp
Salt 1/4 tsp
Sugar 400 g
Oil 200 ml
Egg 2
Buttermilk 125 ml
Vanilla essence 1 tsp

ROSE CUSTARD
Milk 1.2 l
Sugar 240 g
Rose syrup 120 ml
Cornflour 80 g
Glass noodles 60 g

RASPBERRY JELLY
Raspberry puree 700 ml
Sugar 60 g
Gelatin 1/2 tbsp
Warm water 30 ml

CHIA SEEDS JELLY
Chia seeds 30 g
Water 500 ml
Sugar 150 g
Gelatin 1/2 tbsp
Warm water 30 ml

* Preheat the oven to 180°C. Grease a 7-inch round springform pan.

* Soak the chia seeds in cold water for 2 hours.

* For the sponge, sift the flour, baking soda, baking powder and salt together in a bowl.

* In another bowl, whisk the eggs for 5 minutes on high speed, till light and fluffy.

* Lower the speed and add 400 g sugar, oil, buttermilk and vanilla essence. Add the flour mixture and mix on low until combined.

* Spread the batter evenly on the greased springform pan. Tap the pan to ensure the batter is evenly spread and reaches the edges.

* Bake for 17 to 20 minutes or until the cake springs back when you press it. Allow the sponge to cool completely and chill for 2 hours.

* For the rose custard, bring water to a boil in a saucepan and add the glass noodles. Cook for 5 to 6 minutes and then rinse the noodles in cold water. Set aside.

* In a heavy-bottomed saucepan, heat milk, 240 g sugar and rose syrup. Take 2 tablespoons of warm milk and mix it with the cornflour. Add the cornflour mixture to the milk and whisk. Reduce the heat and cook for 3 to 4 minutes, whisking continually. It should thicken slightly.

* Take the pan off the heat and allow it to cool.

* Add glass noodles to the custard and mix to incorporate.

FOR GARNISH

Whipped cream 160 g
Fresh mixed berries
100 g

* To make the raspberry jelly, dissolve the gelatin in warm water and set aside.

* In a medium-sized saucepan, mix the raspberry puree and sugar and bring to a boil.

* Add the gelatin and mix it well. Set aside. (Alternatively, you can use a packet mix of raspberry jelly and follow instructions on how to make it.)

* To make the chia seed jelly, dissolve the gelatin in warm water and allow it to bloom.

* Combine the soaked chia seeds, sugar and gelatin, and set aside.

* To Assemble

* In a large trifle bowl, add a layer of vanilla sponge, followed by a 1 1/2-inch-thick layer of custard and allow it to set in the fridge for 20 minutes.

* Once the custard is set, pour the raspberry jelly mixture till it's about an inch thick. Allow the dessert to set for a further 30 minutes.

* Add another layer of custard over the jelly and chill for 30 minutes till the custard sets.

* Pour the chia seed jelly on top of the custard and allow it to set in the fridge for 15 to 20 minutes.

* Transfer the whipped cream into a piping bag fitted with a plain round nozzle. Pipe dollops of whipped cream on the top of the trifle.

* Garnish with mixed berries.

If you want to speed up the chilling process since the setting time can be quite long, chill the trifle in the freezer for 15 minutes in between each layer. The only disadvantage here is that you will need to keep the trifle out for about 20 to 30 minutes to bring it back to the right serving temperature, and not all layers will be at the same temperature. That's why I prefer doing this the longer way.

Mysore Pak & Tender Coconut Domes

Made with besan and ghee, Mysore Pak is a rich mithai. When paired with tender coconut, it transforms into a surprisingly light concoction.

SERVES 6

INGREDIENTS
BASE
Flour 150 g
Icing sugar 100 g
Unsalted butter 100 g
Mysore pak 300 g
Fresh cream 30 g

MOUSSE
Whipped cream 200 g
White chocolate 100 g
Gelatin 1/2 tbsp
Warm water 40 ml
Coconut milk powder 50 g
Tender coconut pieces, 2-inch size 50 g

GLAZE
White chocolate 100 g
Fresh cream 100 g
Gelatine 1/2 tbsp
Warm water 40 ml
A few drops of white & pink food colouring gel

GARNISH
Chopped pistachios

You can use an array of colours for the glaze. Instead of pistachios, use crushed rose petals, cookie or cake crumbs, or gold leaf for a fancier garnish.

* Preheat the oven to 160°C.

* To make the cookie base, beat the butter and icing sugar till pale in colour and softened. Add the flour to make a dough. Chill in the fridge for 15 to 20 minutes.

* Roll out the dough about 1/2-inch thick. Using a 6-cm round cookie cutter, cut discs. Bake for 12 to 14 minutes.

* In a separate mixing bowl, crush the Mysore pak and mix with the fresh cream. Roll out the mixture and cut with a 6-cm round cutter. Set aside.

* For the mousse, melt white chocolate over a double boiler. Dissolve the gelatin in warm water, add to the chocolate and mix gently.

* Cool the chocolate and fold in the whipped cream. Add the coconut milk powder and tender coconut to make a mousse.

* Pour the mousse into half sphere silicon moulds and set in the fridge for 4 hours.

* To make the glaze, dissolve ½ tbsp gelatin in warm water and set aside. In a saucepan, heat the fresh cream to a simmer. Add the gelatin, then pour the cream over a bowl of white chocolate. Let it sit for a minute before stirring till smooth.

* Take 2 tbsp of glaze in a small bowl and add the white food colouring, then a few drops of pink, to it and set aside.

* Unmould the mousse from the silicon moulds. Lift the mousse with a metal spatula over the bowl of glaze and pour the glaze with a spoon over the mousse till it's evenly coated. Take a teaspoon and lightly splatter the pink glaze over the tops of the mousse. Place on a wire rack to allow any extra glaze to drip off. Coat the edges with chopped pistachios.

* To assemble, take the cookie disc and top with a disc of Mysore pak, followed by the glazed mousse dome.

Jamun Frangipane Tart

Though an unconventional seasonal fruit to use in a dessert, the tangy jamnus perfectly balance this velvety sweet dish.

SERVES 6

INGREDIENTS

TART BASE
Icing sugar 10 g
Flour 200 g
Salt 1/4 tsp
Unsalted butter, chilled
100 g
Baking powder 1/2 tsp
Chilled water 20 ml

FILLING
Almond powder 100 g
Castor sugar 100 g
Butter 100 g
Eggs 2
Kala jamun fruit,
deseeded and roughly
chopped 300 g

GARNISH
Icing sugar (optional)

Jamuns are seasonal, but you can make this tart through the year using other stone fruits like apricots, cherries, peaches or plums.

* Preheat the oven to 180°C and grease a 7-inch rectangular fluted tart tin.

* For the tart dough, sift the flour, icing sugar, baking powder and salt in a bowl.

* Chop the butter into smaller pieces and add to the flour mixture. Gently rub the butter into the flour till it resembles breadcrumbs. Add chilled water and bring the dough together. Add the water in batches, you may not need all 20 ml.

* Turn the dough out onto a lightly floured surface. Knead briefly till smooth and flatten into a disc. Wrap with cling film and chill for an hour.

* Roll out the dough out into a rectangle, about 1/8-inch, keeping 8 inches more on each side so that it's larger than the tin.

* Press the dough along the bottom and sides of the tin. Cut off the excess and chill the base in the fridge for 20 minutes. To blind bake, prick the bottom with a fork and cover with a sheet of parchment paper. Fill with dried beans and bake until the base is set, about 15 minutes.

* Remove the parchment paper and beans and bake until the base is light brown, about 10 minutes.

* For the frangipane filling, combine butter and sugar in a bowl and whisk till creamy. Add the almond flour and then slowly add the eggs, one at a time, whisking between each addition.

* Mix 150 g of jamun in the frangipane filling.

* Pour the frangipane filling into the tart shell and put the remaining jamuns on top.

* Bake for 20 to 25 minutes. Remove the tart from the oven and allow to cool completely and then unmould. Before serving, dust the tart with icing sugar.

Ghevar Apple Crumble

Ghevar, a Rajasthani delicacy made with flour, ghee and milk, replaces the pie shell in this crumble recipe. The ghevar's crispy, porous texture is a perfect match for the tender baked apples.

SERVES 8

INGREDIENTS
Ghevar, approximately
sized 6-inches 1
Red apples 2
Unsalted butter 20 g
Brown sugar 30 g
Cashewnuts, halved
30 g
Raisins 30 g
Cinnamon powder
1/2 tsp

CRUMBLE
Unsalted butter,
cold 40 g
Castor sugar 50 g
Flour 50 g
Cinnamon powder
1/2 tsp

GARNISH
Chopped pistachios

❋ Preheat the oven to 150°C.

❋ Cut the apples into medium-sized wedges, leaving the skin on.

❋ In a saucepan, sauté the apple wedges with butter and 1/2 tsp cinnamon powder for 5 minutes. Add the raisins and cashewnuts and take the saucepan off the heat.

❋ Place the ghevar on a baking tray lightly greased with butter or ghee. Layer the glazed apple mix inside the ghevar and set it aside.

❋ To make the crumble, in a mixing bowl sieve the flour and 1/2 tsp cinnamon powder. Chop the chilled butter and add it to the bowl. Use your fingertips to quickly and lightly rub the flour and butter together until it resembles fine breadcrumbs. Set some aside for the garnish.

❋ Spoon the crumble over the apples and bake for 13 to 16 minutes, or until the crumble is golden brown and the apples have softened.

❋ Garnish with the leftover crumble and chopped pistachios.

Don't hesitate to completely cover the apples with the crumble. If you prefer a crispier texture, bake the crumble separately for 5 to 7 minutes before covering the fruit and baking further.

Bitter Chocolate Nap Naang

A black rice pudding from Nagaland, my version of
Nap Naang is made with dark chocolate to keep it super
healthy. You can even skip the sugar!

SERVES 6

INGREDIENTS
Black rice 120 g
Water 200 ml
Milk 500 ml
Sugar 100 g (optional)
Dark chocolate 120 g
Cardamom powder
1/2 tsp

GARNISH
Whipped cream

✸ Was the black rice a few times and soak it overnight in water.

✸ Drain the rice and cook it in a pressure cooker in 200 ml water for 4 or 5 whistles. Release the pressure from the cooker.

✸ Transfer the rice to a medium-sized saucepan and add milk, sugar and cardamom. Simmer for 10 minutes.

✸ Meanwhile, melt the dark chocolate over a double boiler.

✸ Add the rice mix to the melted chocolate. Pour the rice and chocolate into glasses or any bowl you choose to set the pudding in.

✸ Once cool, refrigerate for 3 to 4 hours. Serve garnished with whipped cream.

To make this dessert sugar-free you can use agave syrup or stevia, or leave it out altogether. The black rice sets this dessert so you don't need to add any gelatin or agar-agar.

Rasmalai & Elaneer Pudding

The mild, sweet flavour of this traditional pudding from Kerala goes wonderfully well with rasmalai, my favourite Indian dessert. It's a happy coupling of north and south.

SERVES 4

INGREDIENTS
PUDDING
Malai from 2 tender
coconuts
Condensed milk 70 g
Rasmalai milk 250 ml
Castor sugar 15 g
(optional)
Rasmalai 4 pieces

FOR MELTING CHINA
GRASS
China grass (agar-agar)
1/2 tbsp
Tender coconut water
250 ml

GARNISH
Tender coconut, thinly-
sliced, oven roasted

⁕ Before you start, decide how you want to set your pudding and keep the glass dish ready. I would recommend individual servings in glasses of different shapes.

⁕ Scoop out the flesh from the tender coconut. Make sure you use a young coconut with soft, tender pulp. Roughly chop the tender coconut flesh and set aside in a bowl.

⁕ In a heavy-bottomed saucepan, combine the rasmalai milk and condensed milk. Bring this to a simmer, and keep stirring to ensure that the milk doesn't burn.

⁕ Taste the mixture and, depending on how sweet you like your dessert, add sugar if required.

⁕ Take this mixture off the heat and pour it over the chopped tender coconut flesh.

⁕ In a clean saucepan, take the tender coconut water and shredded china grass and heat. Stir till the china grass has completely dissolved and take off the heat. Add the tender coconut flesh mixture to this and stir quickly.

⁕ Pour the mixture going half way up the glass. Add chopped pieces of rasmalai, then top off with more mixture. Chill in the fridge for an hour till it sets.

⁕ Garnish with roasted coconut slices or pieces before serving.

Brandy Snap Cannolis with Bhapa Doi

A dessert that puts a tasty twist on sweetened curd. Crunchy and creamy, you won't be able to stop at one.

SERVES 15

INGREDIENTS
CANNOLIS
Castor sugar 27 g
Butter 27 g
Liquid glucose 22 g
Flour 27 g
Brandy 10 ml

BHAPA DOI CREAM
Bhapa doi 300 g
Whipped cream 40 g

GARNISH
Dark chocolate, melted
100 g
Fresh pistachios,
chopped 100 g

✳ Preheat the oven to 170°C.

✳ To make the cannolis, combine the sugar, butter and liquid glucose in a small saucepan and heat till the butter melts and the sugar dissolves. Remove from heat and allow to cool slightly.

✳ Stir in the brandy. Add the flour and mix to form a paste.

✳ Place a silicon mat on a baking tray and drop 2 to 3 teaspoons of mixture onto the tray. Leave enough space to spread the mixture into 1-mm discs using the back of a spoon.

✳ Bake the discs for 5 to 6 minutes until golden brown and remove from oven.

✳ Let the discs cool for 8 to 10 seconds before rolling them around the handle of a greased wooden spoon to shape into cannolis.

✳ Once dry, dip one side of the brandy snap cannolis in melted dark chocolate and then roll in the chopped pistachios. Set aside for the chocolate to set. The brandy snap shells can be stored at room temperature in an airtight container.

✳ For the filling, whip the bhapa doi till soft and fold in the whipped cream. Fill the mixture in a piping bag. The filling can keep for 3 days in the fridge.

✳ At the time of serving, pipe the filling inside the brandy snap cannolis.

If your mixture is on the runny side, pop the bowl into the fridge until it hardens slightly. The consistency of bhapa doi varies (some brands have a much thicker texture) so adjust the amount of whipped cream to ensure the mixture is a pipeable consistency.

Masala Chai Crème Brûlée

A fresh spin on a classic French dessert, the rich custard of this brulee is flavoured with the spicy tones of desi tea.

SERVES 6

INGREDIENTS
Milk 500 ml
Cream 500 g
Masala chai powder
1/2 tbsp
Regular tea powder 10 g
Egg yolks 8
Vanilla essence 10 ml
Castor sugar 200 g
Granulated sugar 100 g

✳ Preheat the oven to 160°C.

✳ In a medium-sized, heavy-based saucepan, heat the milk and cream together. Add the masala chai and tea powders and simmer for 5 to 6 minutes.

✳ Remove from the heat and cover the pan. Allow it to cool for 15 minutes, letting the tea steep.

✳ Meanwhile, whisk the egg yolks and castor sugar together until the mixture is a pale yellow.

✳ Strain the milk and cream. Gradually whisk the egg and sugar mixture into it, adding a little at a time. Add the vanilla essence and whisk it again.

✳ Pour the custard into 6 (7 to 8 ounce) greased ramekins. Place the ramekins in a large cake or roasting pan and pour hot water into the pan. It should come halfway up the sides of the ramekins.

✳ Bake for 40 to 45 minutes, just until the crème brûlée sets but is still wobbly in the centre.

✳ Remove the ramekins from the roasting pan and refrigerate for at least 2 hours.

✳ Remove the crème brûlée from the refrigerator at least 30 minutes prior to caramelizing the top layer.

✳ To finish the dessert, divide the granulated sugar equally among the 6 ramekins, spreading a thin layer evenly over the top. Using a blow torch, caramelize the sugar to crisp the top.

Layer the sugar on top just before you are ready to serve. You can flavour the granulated sugar by grinding a dried vanilla pod and adding it to the sugar to make vanilla sugar. The crème brûlée can stay refrigerated up to 3 days.

Malai Chop Sandwich

These darling little 'sandwiches' are a delicious addition to an afternoon tea tiered stand.

SERVES 6

INGREDIENTS

SPONGE
Refined flour 110 g
Baking soda 1/2 tsp
Baking powder 1/2 tsp
Salt 1/4 tsp
Sugar 200 g
Oil 100 ml
Egg 1
Buttermilk 63 ml
Vanilla essence 1/2 tsp
Rose syrup (I use Kalverts) 33 ml

FILLING
Malai chop cream (appx 14 piece malai chop) 650 g
Whipped cream 150 g
Heavy cream 50 g
Rose water 50 ml

GARNISH
Malai chop cubes 150 g
Red currents 100 g
Silver leaf (varq) for garnish

* Preheat the oven to 180°C. Grease a 8x8-inch square sheet tray with butter and line with butter paper.

* In a mixing bowl, sift the flour, baking soda, baking powder and salt together.

* In another bowl, whisk the egg for 5 minutes on high speed till it's light and fluffy.

* Lower the speed and add sugar, oil, buttermilk, vanilla and rose syrup till combined. Stop whisking and add the dry ingredients, then whisk on low speed until the batter is mixed well.

* Pour the batter into the greased baking tray. Tap the baking tray to ensure batter is evenly spread and reaches the corners.

* Bake for 17 to 20 minutes or until the cake springs back when you press it.

* Allow the sponge to cool completely and chill for 2 hours.

* Remove the cream portion from the malai chop and put it in a small mixing bowl. Cut the malai chop into cubes and set aside to use as garnish.

* To make the filling, mix the malai cream with heavy cream. Fold in the whipped cream and rose water. Transfer the filling into a piping bag fitted with a round nozzle.

* To assemble, slice the sponge horizontally into two even layers. Then cut each layer into triangles.

* Pipe the cream diagonally on each triangle and garnish with malai chop cubes, red currants and silver leaf.

This is a great recipe to make with the kids. Apart from triangles, you can use cookie cutters to make fun sandwich shapes like stars, hearts and flowers.

Amrakhand Mousse & Besan Laddoo Towers

Combine the beauty of mango, white chocolate and besan laddoo to create the ultimate dessert masterpiece.

SERVES 6

INGREDIENTS
Besan laddoo 500 g
Unsalted butter 50 g
White chocolate 100 g

MOUSSE
Amrakhand 600 g
Whipped cream 100 g
Gelatin 1 tsp
Warm water 20 ml

GARNISH
Fresh raspberries 200 g

I like the combination of amrakhand with the besan laddoo but you can experiment with different types of barfis and laddoos that can be broken down into a crumble.

* Crush the besan laddoo to a crumble using a rolling pin. Add the unsalted butter and mix well.

* Place the mixture between two sheets of baking paper. Roll the crumble into a thin layer and refriegerate for 20 to 25 minutes.

* Melt the white chocolate over a double boiler and set it aside.

* Take the rolled laddoo out of the fridge and cut it into discs using a 3-inch round cutter. You will need 18 discs.

* Using a pastry brush, spread a thin layer of melted white chocolate on one side of the discs. Refrigerate the chocolate-covered discs for 30 minutes.

* Melt the gelatin in warm water, and set aside.

* Scoop the amrakhand into a mixing bowl. Loosen it by adding a spoonful of whipped cream.

* Gently fold the rest of the whipped cream into the amrakhand and add the gelatin. Give it a quick stir to incorporate the gelatin evenly. (Too much whisking will knock the air out of the whipped cream.)

* Transfer the mousse into a piping bag fitted with a roun nozzle.

* To layer the towers, take a besan disc (white chocolate side down) and pipe peaks of mousse. Place another besan disc on top and repeat the layers. You need 3 layers each of disc and mousse.

* Set in the fridge for an hour. Garnish with fresh raspberries or mixed berries and serve.

Pista Barfi, Cranberry & Oatmeal Bars

These oatmeal bars, with a rich, nutty barfi base, are a delicious snack for both adults and kids.

MAKES 10 BARS

INGREDIENTS
Pista barfi 500 g
Cornflakes 60 g
White oats 100 g
Toasted sunflower seeds 100 g
Golden syrup 75 ml
Maple syrup 75 ml
White chocolate 50 g
Dried cranberries 50 g

✳ Line an 8x8-inch sheet tray with butter paper. Make a layer of pista barfi on the tray and chill in the fridge for 15 to 20 minutes.

✳ Combine the maple syrup and golden syrup in a saucepan and heat over a medium flame until it comes to simmer, stirring occasionally. Set it aside.

✳ Melt the white chocolate in a microwave. Remove, then stir in the maple and golden syrup mixture and combine well.

✳ Add all the dry ingredient to the syrup mixture. Once the granola is well combined, layer the mixture on top of the pista barfi. Spread it evenly and press the granola down on top of the barfi.

✳ Cover the tray with cling film refrigerate for 2 hours.

✳ Unmould the slab and cut into even rectangular bars. Store in an airtight container in the fridge for up to a week. Bring the bars to room temperature before eating.

Choose a pista barfi with a coarser texture which gives these bars their chewy texture. The barfi should still have pieces of pista in it and not be ground into a smooth paste.

Aamras & Malibu Tiramisu

My boozy take on a classic tiramisu, this mango and coconut concoction is an explosion of fruity flavours.

SERVES 8

INGREDIENTS
Egg yolk 3
Castor sugar 45 g
Mascarpone cheese 180 g
Vanilla essence 1 tsp
Whipped cream 120 g
Mango puree 120 g
Alphonso mango cubes 500 g
Ladyfingers 200 g packet

SYRUP
Water 300 ml
Sugar 90 g
Malibu liqueur 60 ml

✳ In a medium-sized bowl, whisk the egg yolks and castor sugar over a double boiler until creamy. Add vanilla essence and continue whisking until the mixture goes from a bright to a pale yellow.

✳ In another bowl, lightly whisk the mascarpone till smooth. Gently fold in the egg yolk mixture, followed by whipped cream and mango puree. Transfer it into piping bag and chill.

✳ To make the Malibu syrup, combine water and sugar in a saucepan and bring it to a simmer. Stir well, until the sugar has dissolved, and allow it to cool. Add the Malibu liqueur and set it aside.

✳ Soak each ladyfinger biscuit in the Malibu syrup for 1 to 2 seconds and layer them evenly in a 6x6-inch glass dish.

✳ Pipe the aamras mascarpone over the layer of ladyfinger. Use a flat spatula to even it out.

✳ Add an even layer of chopped mangoes over the mascarpone.

✳ Arrange another layer of Malibu-soaked ladyfingers on top, followed by the aamras mascarpone.

✳ For the topmost layer, pipe the aamras mascarpone in diagonal lines.

✳ Refrigerate for a few hours before serving.

You can use sliced mangoes to garnish this dessert and pack in some extra mango flavour. For a child-friendly version of this dessert, just omit the Malibu.

Ravo Tiramisu

A Parsi version of kheer, the ravo recipe I use was given to me by a Parsi family friend and blends beautifully with the dark chocolate.

SERVES 6

INGREDIENTS

RAVO LAYER
Suji (semolina) 60 g
Milk, warmed 500 ml
Castor sugar 100 g
Butter 20 g
Cardamom powder
1/2 tsp

CHOCOLATE CREAM LAYER
Egg yolks 3
Castor sugar 45 g
Mascarpone cheese
180 g
Vanilla essence 1 tsp
Whipped cream 120 g
Melted dark chocolate
200 g

SUGAR SYRUP
Water 100 ml
Sugar 30 g

GARNISH
Whipped cream 120 g
Ladyfinger 400 g
Cocoa powder to dust

You can create individual servings of this dessert by layering glasses or bowls. Better yet, make mini tiramisus by building ring-shaped layers.

✳ Make the ravo by melting butter in a heavy-bottomed saucepan. Add the suji and cook until light brown. Then, add the warmed milk, cardamom powder and sugar and cook for 10 to 12 minutes, stirring with a wooden spoon. Set aside to cool.

✳ For the chocolate cream, in a medium-sized bowl whip the egg yolks and castor sugar together over a double boiler to cook out the egg yolk. Add vanilla essence and continue whisking until the mixture goes from bright yellow to pale yellow. Allow to cool.

✳ In another bowl soften the mascarpone by whipping on low speed. Gently fold in the egg yolk mixture.

✳ Add the melted chocolate and whisk manually to incorporate.

✳ Fold in the whipped cream and set aside.

✳ Make a sugar syrup by dissolving sugar in hot water. Set aside to cool.

✳ Take a 7-inch round cake ring and place it on a cake board. Alternatively, you can wrap the base with cling film.

✳ Dip the ladyfingers in the sugar syrup and layer them evenly on the base of the ring.

✳ Pour an even layer of chocolate cream, about 1-inch high, over the ladyfingers and freeze for 5 to 7 minutes.

✳ Top the chocolate cream layer with a layer of ravo and freeze for 5 to 7 minutes, or until the ravo is firm to the touch. Repeat the layers, then chill the dessert for an hour in the fridge.

✳ To unmould the tiramisu, use a blowtorch to evenly heat the sides of the ring, using just enough heat to loosen the layers.

✳ Cut ladyfinger biscuits into 7-cm pieces and line the sides of the tiramisu. Pipe whipped cream on top of the tiramisu and dust with cocoa powder before serving.

Shahi Tukda Cinnamon Rolls with Rabri Cream

My spin on the Hyderabadi fried-bread dessert, these rolls are super easy to make, and lighter and crispier than churros.

SERVES 6

INGREDIENTS

Bread slice, large 6 pieces
Unsalted butter, softened 100 g
Cinnamon powder 10 g
Castor sugar 200 g
Ghee for frying
Rabri 300 g

✳ Cut the crusts off the slices of bread. Using a rolling pin, lightly flatten the bread slices.

✳ In a bowl, cream the butter with cinnamon powder and sugar. The mixture should increase in volume and turn a paler colour.

✳ Spread the cinnamon butter generously on each slice of bread and roll the slice like you would a Swiss roll.

✳ Allow all the rolled bread slices to set in the fridge for 2 hours.

✳ Slice each roll horizontally to create individual swirls.

✳ Thread the swirls with a wooden skewer so they don't unravel when fried.

✳ Heat ghee in a deep saucepan, pouring enough to immerse the swirls.

✳ Deep-fry the bread swirls till golden brown, then drain on a paper towel.

✳ In a bowl, combine the castor sugar and cinnamon. Toss the warm swirls in the cinnamon sugar, then remove the skewers. Serve warm, with warmed rabri.

You can also serve these with chocolate sauce, cinnamon butter sauce (Heat liquid glucose, butter, sugar and cinnamon to make it) and even good old vanilla ice cream.

Kala Jamun Bread & Butter Pudding

A treat that packs in all the buttery goodness of an English bread-and-butter pudding, with kala jamuns to add the right amount of sweetness.

SERVES 4

INGREDIENTS

PUDDING
Milk 188 ml
Heavy cream 188 ml
Eggs 2
Egg yolk 1/2
Castor sugar 75 g
Vanilla essence 3 to 4 drops
Butter, salted 30 g
Bread slices, large 5 to 6
Kala jamun 6 pieces, thinly sliced

BOURBON SAUCE
Egg yolks 2
Brown sugar 90 g
Unsalted butter 120 g
Bourbon (I use Jack Daniels) 60 ml
Cinnamon powder Ð tsp
Nutmeg powder Ð tsp

※ Preheat the oven to 150°C and grease a ceramic casserole baking dish with butter.

※ To make the pudding, heat the milk and cream together in a pan.

※ In a large bowl, combine 2 eggs, 1/2 egg yolk and castor sugar. Pour the hot milk and cream mixture over the eggs and stir, allowing the sugar to melt. Add vanilla essence and strain the custard.

※ Butter the slices of bread and cut them into small squares. Arrange the pieces in the baking dish. Pour enough custard to cover the bread and allow it to soak for 10 minutes. Arrange the sliced kala jamuns on top, covering the entire surface.

※ Top with a final layer of bread and custard, allowing the bread to soak up the custard well.

※ Place the pudding dish in a larger square tin and pour hot water in the tin till it comes halfway up the sides of the pan. Bake for 40 minutes or until the centre of the pudding is cooked.

※ To prepare the bourbon sauce, melt the brown sugar and mix in the 2 egg yolks in a steady steam, whisking vigorously.

※ Add the butter, cinnamon and nutmeg. Strain the sauce to catch any bits of cooked egg, and then add the bourbon.

※ Serve the sauce with warm bread pudding.

I would recommend using salted butter for this recipe instead of unsalted. The salt in the butter really brings out the flavour of the spices in the sauce and balances the sweetness of the kala jamuns.

Chees
&

ecakes
Cakes

Aflatoon Cheesecake

A khoya-based baked dessert packed with dry fruits, aflatoon is a delicacy from the Bohri Muslim community. In this creation, aflatoon serves as a base for a cheesecake.

SERVES 8

INGREDIENTS

CRUST
Digestive biscuits 100 g
Unsalted butter, softened 60 g
Granulated sugar 20 g
Aflatoon 300 g

FILLING
Philadelphia cream cheese 400 g
Castor sugar 160 g
Corn flour 40 g
Eggs 4
Vanilla essence 10 ml

GARNISH
Aflatoon 100 g

Don't skip the water bath and bake the cheesecake in a dry oven. A water bath adds moisture to the oven, which is necessary or the cheesecake may crack when exposed to dry heat.

If you don't have a food processor, place the biscuits in a strong plastic bag and crush with a rolling pin.

* Preheat the oven to 180°C.

* In a food processor, pulse the biscuits to a fine crumb. Add the softened butter and pulse until well combined. Add the granulated sugar and pulse again.

* Cover the base of a 9-inch round springform cake tin with silver foil. Make sure the base is smooth and there are no wrinkles in the foil or your cheesecake will not have a smooth base.

* Place the biscuit crumb in the tin and press down to create a crust. Add the 300 g of aflatoon to the ring and press down till smooth and evenly covered. You can use the base of a small steel bowl to ensure a smooth finish. Chill for 30 minutes.

* In a bowl, mix the cream cheese and sugar. Add the cornflour and vanilla, mix well and then add the eggs one by one.

* Scrape the sides of the bowl and mix well again till smooth.

* Pour the batter over the aflatoon base.

* Bake the cheesecake in a water bath (place the cheesecake pan in a larger square tin and pour hot water in the tin till it comes halfway up the sides of the pan).

* Bake for 40 minutes or until the cheesecake is firm along the edges.

* Cool on a wire rack for 10 minutes. Then carefully run a knife around the edge of the tin to loosen it and unlock the springform tin.

* Chill the cheesecake in the fridge for two hours. Unmould and serve, garnished with small circular cut-outs of aflatoon.

Chocolate Barfi Cheesecake

The smooth and creamy texture of chocolate barfi complements cheesecake beautifully. A crowd-pleaser, this dessert is the perfect sweet end to your party.

SERVES 10

INGREDIENTS

CRUST
Digestive biscuits 110 g
Unsalted butter, softened 45 g
Granulated sugar 20 g
Chocolate barfi (only brown layer) 550 g

FILLING
Philadelphia cream cheese 380 g
Castor sugar 75 g
Cornflour 7.5 g
Eggs 2
Vanilla essence 1 tsp
Dark chocolate, roughly chopped 200 g
Heavy cream 175 g

GARNISH
Chocolate barfi 150 g
Roasted almond flakes 20 g

You can have fun with the garnishes. Drizzle a thin ganache, add a dollop of chocolate sauce or stud with chocolate truffles. Try tart fruits like strawberries, raspberries and red currents to add some freshness.

* Preheat the oven to 180 C.

* In a food processor, pulse the biscuits to a fine crumb. Add the softened butter and pulse until mixed. Add the granulated sugar and pulse again.

* Press the crumb mixture onto the bottom of a greased 9-inch springform cake tin.

* If the chocolate barfi you are using is brown and white, cut out the white and only use the brown layer.

* Layer the chocolate barfi over the crumb base. Gently press down to eliminate any gaps.

* In a bowl, mix cream cheese, castor sugar and cornflour, and whisk till smooth. Add the eggs, one at a time, beating well after each addition.

* In a saucepan, heat the cream and bring it to a simmer.

* Pour the warm cream over the chopped chocolate. Let the mixture sit for a minute before stirring till smooth.

* Add vanilla essence to the ganache. Gently fold the cream cheese mixture with the ganache and then pour the batter over the chocolate barfi crust.

* Bake the cheesecake in a water bath (place the cheesecake pan in a larger square tin and pour hot water in the tin till it comes halfway up the sides of the pan). Bake for 45 to 50 minutes or until the centre is set.

* Cool on a wire rack for 10 minutes. Carefully run a knife around edge of the pan to loosen the cheesecake, then cool for 60 minutes longer.

* Garnish with cubes of chocolate barfi and roasted almond flakes.

Raskadam Cheesecake

A soft creamy texture and a juicy centre, the version of the Bengali raskadam that I use for this dessert has a fragrant rose flavour which perfumes this dessert beautifully.

SERVES 10

INGREDIENTS
CRUST
Digestive biscuits 110 g
Unsalted butter, softened 45 g
Granulated sugar 20 g

FILLING
Philadelphia cream cheese 300 g
Whipped cream 300 g
Condensed milk 100 g
Water 2 tbsp
Gelatin 5 g
Raskadam 14 pieces

✳ In a food processor, pulse the biscuits to a fine crumb. Add the softened butter and pulse until well combined. Add the granulated sugar and pulse again.

✳ Press the crumb mixture onto the bottom of a greased 9-inch springform cake tin and chill it in the fridge.

✳ In a bowl, whisk the cream cheese and condensed milk until smooth.

✳ Gently fold the whipped cream into the cheesecake filling. Be careful not to knock out too much air as you want a light cheesecake.

✳ In a small pan, warm the water. Add the gelatin and heat until it dissolves.

✳ Add the gelatin mixture to the cream cheese mixture and mix well.

✳ Pour half the cheesecake batter on top of the crust.

✳ Cut 9 pieces of raskadam into half and layer the mithai over the cheesecake mix. Leave it to set in the fridge for 10 minutes.

✳ Take the chilled cheesecake out of the fridge, then pour the remaining cheesecake batter on top. Use a palate knife to smooth the top, then leave it to set in the fridge overnight.

✳ Before serving, use a knife to loosen the chilled cheesecake from the rim of the springform pan. Garnish with raskadam.

There are many variations of raskadam, so taste a few before deciding on a flavor to use. I usually buy the rose-flavoured one from the Sweet Bengal mithai shop.

Milk Cake Cheesecake

Milk cake is a fudge-type dessert made from caramelizing milk and sugar. In this recipe, the chocolate biscuits balance the sweet creaminess of the dish.

SERVES 10

INGREDIENTS
CRUST
Oreo biscuits 250 g
Unsalted butter, softened 80 g
Granulated sugar 30 g
Milk cake 360 g

FILLING
Philadelphia cream cheese 375 g
Castor sugar 75 g
Heavy cream 150 ml
Cornflour 7.5 g
Eggs 2
Vanilla essence 1 tsp

GARNISH
A few slivered almonds
Few pieces of milk cake, crushed
Powdered sugar (optional)

If you want a sweeter cheesecake, add a second layer of milk cake and batter. You can also serve this cheesecake with saffron milk on the side.

* Preheat the oven to 180°C.

* In a food processor, pulse the Oreos to a fine crumb. Add the softened butter and pulse till well combined. Add the granulated sugar and pulse again.

* Press the crust mixture onto the bottom and around the sides of a 9-inch springform cake tin.

* Add a layer of milk cake and gently press down to eliminate any gaps. Use the base of a small steel bowl to ensure a smooth finish.

* In a bowl, beat the cream cheese, cornflour and sugar till well mixed well.

* Add the eggs, one at a time, beating well after each addition.

* Add the vanilla essence.

* Pour the batter over the milk cake crust.

* Bake the cheesecake in a water bath (place the cheesecake pan in a larger square tin and pour hot water in the tin till it comes halfway up the sides of the pan).

* Bake for 45 to 50 minutes or until the cheesecake is slightly firm in the centre.

* Cool on a wire rack for 10 minutes. Then carefully run a knife around the edge of the tin to loosen it and unlock the springform tin.

* Chill the cheesecake in the fridge for two hours. Unmould and serve, garnished with crushed milk cake, powdered sugar or slivered almonds.

Red Velvet Swiss Roll with Shrikhand Frosting

This red velvet sponge is my prized recipe. I went through almost 30 different permutations before perfecting it. This Swiss roll is a delicious accompaniment to afternoon tea.

SERVES 10

INGREDIENTS

CAKE

Refined flour 220 g
Castor sugar 400 g
Baking soda $1/2$ tsp
Baking powder $1/2$ tsp
Salt $1/2$ tsp
Cocoa powder 30 g
Oil 200 ml
Egg 2
Buttermilk 200 ml
Vanilla essence 1 tsp
A few drops of red food colouring gel
White vinegar 1 tsp
Coffee powder 2 tsp

FROSTING

Shrikhand 500 g
Whipped cream 100 g

You can use this recipe to bake a regular cake or cupcakes with either a shrikhand or cream cheese frosting. Buttercream works too, but a tart frosting will balance the flavour.

❋ Preheat the oven to 180°C. Grease a 13x9-inch baking tin with butter and line with butter paper.

❋ Sift the flour, baking soda, baking powder, salt and cocoa powder together.

❋ In another bowl, using a hand whisk, beat the eggs for 5 minutes on high speed till light and fluffy.

❋ Lower the speed and add sugar, oil, buttermilk, vinegar, vanilla, food colouring and coffee powder to the beaten eggs. Mix till combined well. The colour of your batter should be a vibrant red.

❋ Add the dry flour mixture and whisk on low speed. The batter will be on the wetter side but that makes for a light sponge.

❋ Spread the batter evenly on the baking tray and bake for 17 to 20 minutes or until the cake springs back when you press it. Allow the sponge to cool and chill in the fridge for two hours.

❋ To make the frosting, gently fold the shrikhand into the whipped cream. Chill in the fridge.

❋ Unmould the sponge and peel off the butter paper. Place the sponge on a fresh piece of butter paper that is larger in size.

❋ Spread the frosting evenly on top, leaving an inch clear around the edges as the frosting will spread when you roll the cake.

❋ Gently start rolling the cake. Use the butter paper to keep the roll tight. Take the paper between your index finger and thumb, and use the rest of your fingers to push the roll over.

❋ Chill in the fridge for three to four hours to set. Slice it at the time of serving.

Brown Butter, Rose & Chai Cake

This is one of those cakes that will end up becoming a rainy day family favourite. It's best enjoyed with a cup of tea.

SERVES 10

INGREDIENTS
CAKE
Flour 228 g
Baking powder $^1/_4$ tsp
Baking soda 1 tsp
Salt 1 tsp
Cardamom powder
$^1/_2$ tsp
Yogurt 160 g
Castor sugar 200 g
Oil 130 ml
Rose water 1 tsp
Black tea leaves (use a brand like Society) 2 $^1/_2$ tbsp
Milk 165 ml

GLAZE
Unsalted butter 60 g
Icing sugar 180 g
Cardamom powder
$^1/_2$ tsp
Rose essence 2 ml
Milk 2 tbsp

This cake looks stunning garnished with dried rose buds or even sugared flowers.

* Preheat the oven to 170°C. Line and grease a 8.5x4.5 loaf pan.

* Brew the tea with 165 ml milk first. Bring it to a boil, remove from the heat and keep it covered for 3 to 4 minutes to allow the tea to steep. Strain with a fine mesh sieve and bring the milk tea to room temperature before using. You need around 2/3 cup of tea.

* Sift the flour, baking powder, baking soda, salt and cardamom powder together and set aside.

* In a large mixing bowl, whisk the yogurt and sugar for a few minutes. Add the oil and rose water and whisk for another few minutes till the mixture is creamy.

* Add the sifted dry ingredients and the milk tea to the batter. Gently fold in the dry ingredients with a spatula. Pour into the greased loaf tin and bake for 35 to 40 minutes.

* While the cake bakes, make the glaze. Sift the icing sugar and cardamom powder together and set aside.

* Cook the butter in a saucepan over a low flame for 5 to 8 minutes till the butter browns. Be careful not to burn the butter. Strain the browned butter to remove any impurities.

* Add the icing sugar, a little at a time, and whisk to combine. Add a few teaspoons of milk and rose essence to thin the glaze, so it's a pourable consistency.

* Remove the tea cake from the oven and allow it to cool completely on a wire rack. Carefully run a knife around edge of the pan to loosen before unmoulding.

* Once the cake is completely cooled, drizzle the glaze on top.

Lavender & Darjeeling Tea Cake

My son loves this cake! Every time he takes a bite of this
subtly sweet, delicate tea cake he runs around saying 'Mmm'.
That's all the validation I need to know this recipe is a hit.

SERVES 8

INGREDIENTS
Milk 125 ml
Darjeeling tea bags 3
Unsalted butter 114 g
Castor sugar 4 tsp
Eggs 2
Vanilla essence 1 tsp
Flour 180 g
Baking powder 1 tsp
Salt 1/2 tsp
Loose Darjeeling tea
1 tsp
Lavender extract 2 tsp

GLAZE
Icing sugar 100 g
Milk 3 tbsp
Soft butter 2 tbsp
Lavender extract 2
drops
Vanilla essence 2 drops
Lavender food colouring
gel 1 drop

GARNISH
A few lavender buds

* Gently warm the milk. Take it off the heat and add the 3 tea
  bags. Cover and let it steep for 30 to 40 minutes. Squeeze the
  tea bags and discard.

* Preheat the oven to 180°C and grease a 7-inch bundt cake tin.

* Whisk the flour, baking powder, salt and tea leaves together.

* Whisk the butter and sugar in a separate bowl until creamy.
  Add the eggs one at a time, beating between additions,
  followed by the vanilla essence.

* Add the dry ingredients to the wet batter and mix well, then
  add the milk tea concoction.

* Pour the batter into the bundt cake tin and bake for
  25 minutes. Remove from the oven and allow it to cool
  completely on a wire rack. Unmould the cake before glazing.

* For the glaze, whisk the icing sugar, butter, milk, lavender and
  vanilla essence together to a thick consistency. Then add the
  lavender food colouring gel.

* Pour the glaze over the tea cake, and sprinkle lavender buds
  as garnish.

*Don't glaze the cake till you are ready to serve. Once the glaze is set at room temperature, store the cake in
an airtight container in a cool room.*

Gajar Ka Halwa Cake

A modern spin on a slow-cooked Indian classic, this is the perfect cake for a New Age Indian wedding. The cream cheese cuts through the halwa's heaviness creating a dessert that's both light and luscious.

SERVES 30

INGREDIENTS

HALWA

Carrots, peeled and grated 750 g
Ghee 20 g
Milk 750 ml
Castor sugar 12 tbsp
Cardamom powder 2 tsp
Butter 3 tbsp

CAKE

Gajar ka halwa 1.4 kg
Flour 1.2 kg
Baking powder 60 g
Salt 10 g
Castor sugar 256 g
Whole milk 1.5 litres
Vegetable oil 224 ml
Vanilla essence 2 tbsp

FROSTING

Philadelphia Cream Cheese 1 kg
Unsalted butter 500 g
Icing sugar 500 g
Cardamom powder 1 tsp
Vanilla essence 2 tbsp

❋ To make the gajar ka halwa, take half the ghee in a large, heavy-bottomed pan. Make sure your pan is wide enough.

❋ Add the grated carrots and cook. Keep stirring and cooking till the water from the carrots evaporates.

❋ Add the milk, sugar and the remaining ghee. Cook until all the milk is absorbed by the carrots. The carrots should be soft but still have a slight bite. This adds texture to the cake and keeps it moist.

❋ Add the cardamom powder and butter, and mix.

❋ To make the sponge cake, preheat the oven to 175°C and grease two round baking tins (7-inch and 4-inch) and keep aside.

❋ In a bowl, mix the flour, baking powder, salt and sugar.

❋ Add milk, oil, vanilla essence and mix until everything comes together. Do not overmix the batter.

❋ Fold in the cooled gajar ka halwa till well mixed.

❋ Pour the batter into both greased cake tins and fill about half or three-fourth of the pans. Bake for about 50 minutes to one hour. The centre of the cakes should be firm and a tooth pick should come out clean when inserted. Allow them to cool down completely on a wire rack.

❋ Prepare the frosting while the cakes are cooling. In a bowl beat the cream cheese, butter and icing sugar till softened and blended. Add the vanilla essence and cardamom powder, and mix well.

SALTED CARAMEL DRIZZLE (OPTIONAL)

Granulated sugar 2 cup
Salted butter, room temperature 12 tbsp
Heavy cream 1 cup

❋ Slice the cakes horizontally into two even layers. Using a spatula, frost the layers of both cakes so you have cake, frosting, cake and frosting. Cover the sides of both cakes with frosting. If you want to create a 'naked cake effect', use a cake scraper to brush the sides of the cake till the frosting is smooth but parts of the cake are still visible. Then place the smaller cake on the larger cake. Chill for an hour.

❋ For the salted caramel drizzle, heat the sugar in a saucepan on medium-low for about five minutes. Use a spatula to occasionally stir the sugar, scraping the bottom of the pan. Once all of the sugar has fully melted and turned a medium gold colour, take the pan off the heat and quickly stir in the butter. The mixture will bubble violently, but that's okay. Use a spatula to stir the butter and sugar until combined. Pour in the heavy cream and stir until you get a smooth mixture. Place the pan back on the stove for about 30 seconds, stirring the whole time. Remove from the heat and allow to cool for 15 minutes.

❋ Pour the caramel over the top of the cake, in a circular motion, and use the back of a spoon to help pull the caramel down the sides of the cake to create a drizzle effect.

I prefer not to use khoya in my gajar ka halwa recipe, which makes it lighter than the traditional halwa. I use red winter carrots when in season as the colour and flavour are more intense compared to the orange carrots that are available year-round. You can, of course, always use store-bought gajar ka halwa.

T

ruffles

Kaju Katli Truffles

Kaju katli is one of my favourite mithais to indulge in. I can go through about 12 of these in one sitting! The truffle's chewy, soft, cashew-rich centre pairs perfectly with a dark chocolate shell.

MAKES 12 PIECES

INGREDIENTS
Kaju katli 200 g
Cream cheese 20 g

COATING
Dark chocolate 100 g

GARNISH
Silver leaf (varq)

❋ Chop the kaju katli into small pieces and using the back of a spoon or a fork, gently mash it. Ensure the mithai is at a room temperature so that it mashes easily.

❋ Add a little bit of cream cheese to loosen the kaju katli pieces. Then stir in the remaining cream cheese until it forms an even paste. Store in the fridge for approximately 30 minutes.

❋ Measure 15 g of the filling for each truffle (10 g for smaller truffles) and roll into even balls. Transfer these to a tray, cover with cling film and set them in the freezer for 10 minutes.

❋ Melt the dark chocolate over a double boiler. Stir at intervals to make sure the chocolate melts evenly without any lumps. Set aside.

❋ Take the truffle balls out from the fridge and, using a skewer, dip each truffle into the melted dark chocolate until coated completely. Lift it out and let the excess chocolate drip off.

❋ Place the coated truffles on baking paper and place in the fridge to set.

❋ Garnish with silver leaf once the truffles have set. These truffles can be stored in the fridge for up to 3 days.

For a makeshift double boiler, place a small, flat-bottomed bowl over a larger pan of simmering water. Ensure there is a gap between the water level and the bottom of the insert so that any bowl you place on top of the double boiler is heated by the steam, and not the hot water.

Maghai Paan Truffles

Reimagining a classic mouth freshener, I created these truffles to be served as an after-dinner mint that even children can enjoy.

MAKES 12 PIECES

INGREDIENTS
Paan leaves, finely
chopped 2
Heavy cream 80 g
Gulkand 60 g
White chocolate 140 g

COATING
White chocolate 100 g
Desiccated coconut
40 g

GARNISH
Dried rose petals 10 g

❊ In a heavy-bottomed saucepan, heat the cream and add the paan leaves. Simmer for 4 to 5 minutes, then take the pan off the heat. Cover with a lid, and let it steep for around 15 minutes.

❊ In a double boiler, melt 140 g white chocolate till completely smooth.

❊ Take the chocolate off the heat, stir in the infused cream and mix well. Once cool, cover with cling film and refrigerate for 30 minutes so that the ganache can be rolled.

❊ Measure 5 g of gulkand for each truffle and roll into balls. Place the balls in the freezer for 10 to 15 minutes to set.

❊ Take the ganache and gulkand balls out of the fridge. Measure 15 g pieces of the ganache and roll into rough balls. Using your finger, make an indent in the centre of the ganache ball and stuff it with the gulkand ball. Cover the gulkand with the ganache and roll into an even ball.

❊ Place all the rolled truffles into the fridge for 10 minutes.

❊ Melt 100 g white chocolate over a double boiler till smooth. Using a skewer, dip the truffles into melted white chocolate and then into desiccated coconut till evenly coated.

❊ Garnish with dried rose petals. These truffles can be stored in the fridge for up to 3 days.

If you don't want to use rose petals as garnish, try edible flower petals that have been crystalized. Brush the petals with a thin coating of egg white and then dip into castor sugar. Set aside to dry before using.

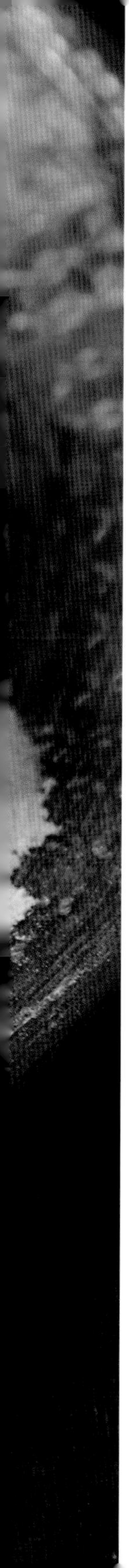

Kesar Peda Truffles

A festive favourite made of saffron, cardamom and rich khoya goes mod with this recipe which is both simple and delicious. A quick-fix for a dinner party when you have very little time to make dessert.

MAKES 12 PIECES

INGREDIENTS

Kesar peda 200 g
Cream cheese 10 g
Icing sugar 10 g

COATING

Powdered sugar 100 g

- Mash the kesar peda in a bowl using the back of a spoon or a fork. Ensure the mithai is at a room temperature so that it mashes easily.
- Add the icing sugar and cream cheese and mix till it forms a paste-like consistency. Refrigerate the filling for approximately 30 minutes.
- Measure 15 g of filling for each truffle and roll into balls.
- Store the truffles in an airtight container in the fridge till you are ready to serve.
- To serve, bring the truffles to room temperature and toss them in powdered sugar. These truffles can keep for a week in the fridge.

These truffles look stunning served on a beautiful silver tray, rolled in powdered sugar. Toss a few strands of saffron into the powdered sugar to create a more dazzling impact.

Date & Cardamom Truffles

Dates and chocolate are a match made in heaven. Add a sprinkling of cool, aromatic elaichi and these truffles will taste simply divine.

MAKES 12 PIECES

INGREDIENTS
Seedless dates 50 g
Heavy cream 800 g
Milk chocolate bar 80 g
Cardamom powder
1/2 tsp

COATING
Milk chocolate bar 100 g

GARNISH
Dark chocolate 20 g
Chopped almonds, or
any nuts of your choice
30 g

* Finely chop the dates.

* In a heavy-bottomed saucepan, bring the heavy cream along with the chopped dates and cardamom powder to a simmer.

* Melt 80 g milk chocolate over a double boiler.

* Take the chocolate off the double boiler and combine with the heavy cream mixture to make a ganache. Cool and refrigerate the ganache for 30 minutes.

* Make even rounds of 15 g each of the cold ganache. Chill in the fridge for 15 minutes.

* Melt 100 g milk chocolate over a double boiler. Dip the ganache balls into the chocolate using a toothpick and coat evenly. Tap to remove excess chocolate. Set aside on a baking sheet and chill in the fridge for 15 to 20 minutes till the chocolate is set.

* Melt 20 g dark chocolate in a double boiler (or microwave) and fill in a piping bag. Pipe straight streams over the truffles. Garnish with chopped almonds. These truffles can be stored in the fridge for up to 3 days.

If you have warm hands like I do, chocolate usually melts on contact with your hands. Either use food grade gloves when rolling the truffles or dip your hands at intervals in ice cold water, pat dry and roll.

Fennel & Star Anise Truffles

Fennel seeds and star anise, known as saunf and chakra phool in Indian kitchens, are similar and strong spices that go beautifully together. Like the Maghai Paan Truffles, they're great to serve after dinner.

MAKES 12 PIECES

INGREDIENTS
Heavy cream 80 g
White chocolate 150 g
Fennel seeds 10 g
Star anise 20 g

COATING
White chocolate 100 g
A few drops of green
food colouring gel

* In a heavy-bottomed saucepan, combine the cream, fennel seeds and star anise and bring to a simmer. Take it off the heat and let it steep for 10 minutes.

* Melt 150 g white chocolate over a double boiler till smooth.

* Strain, then add the cream mixture to the melted chocolate and stir to make a smooth ganache. After it cools, refrigerate the bowl of ganache for 60 minutes.

* Measure 15 g of ganache and roll into balls. Store in the fridge for 15 to 20 minutes.

* Melt the remaining white chocolate over a double boiler and add a few drops of green food colouring so that the chocolate turns a light pistachio green colour. Reserve some white chocolate for the garnish.

* Using a skewer or toothpick, dip the ganache balls into the white chocolate and coat evenly. Tap to remove excess chocolate.

* Transfer the dipped truffles onto a baking sheet and then to the fridge till the chocolate sets.

* Garnish with white chocolate piping. (See Date & Cardamom Truffles pp. 86-87 for how to make piping chocolate.) These truffles can be stored in the fridge for up to 3 days.

You can also use crystalized flower petals as garnish (See Maghai Paan Truffles on p. 82)

...rified and upset m...
... It could hardly h...
...ed to have my smok...
...and given the strong...
...moke would invariably...
...y spoke about it strongly to...
... But I made no promises to...
...derstood that none of the children wou...
nerve to smoke in my father's presence. In fa...
smoking (he quit years ago) remained a well-...
secret till he too was 'caught'. All those years back, the
health ha... ...king was not known in...
such ... ...t carry statutory
w... ...d lung cancer
... ...use it was
... ...was an
... ...uences.
... ...killers.
... ...king,
... ...plete
... ...t in a
... ...ned.
... ...but
... ...han I

114

...est the
... ...e about
... ...want to. I
... ...yself. It's a
p... ...ntly fix most
relax... ...cuse? Sure. There
are definite... ...ys to relax and unwind.
But there it is, my little Achilles' heel, my unfortunate

an...
actu...

Masala Chai Truffles

Brimming with ginger, cinnamon, cardamom, nutmeg, black pepper and cloves – who can resist a hot cup of cutting chai? This truffle recipe captures that kick of spice.

MAKES 12 PIECES

INGREDIENTS
Heavy cream 80 g
Milk chocolate 140 g
Masala chai powder 1/2 tbsp (add more if you like a stronger flavour)

COATING
Milk chocolate 100 g

GARNISH
Crystalized ginger

※ In a heavy-bottomed saucepan, combine the cream and chai powder and bring to a boil. Take the pan off the heat and set it aside to steep for 15 to 20 minutes.

※ Using a fine sieve, strain the cream into a clean saucepan and heat it again till it reaches a low simmer.

※ Roughly chop the milk chocolate and transfer to a separate bowl.

※ Pour the warm cream over the chocolate and stir after a minute until the mixture is smooth.

※ Transfer the bowl with the ganache to the fridge and chill for an hour.

※ Make 15 g balls of the ganache and transfer to a baking sheet. Chill the rolled truffles for 15 minutes in the fridge.

※ Melt 100 g milk chocolate over a double boiler until smooth.

※ Using a toothpick dip the truffles into the chocolate and coat evenly. Tap to remove excess chocolate. Transfer the truffles to a baking sheet and into the fridge to set.

※ Garnish each truffle with a few strands of crystalized ginger before serving. These truffles can be stored in the fridge for up to 3 days.

Crystalized ginger can be made at home. Blanch 680 g ginger juliennes first in hot, then cold, water. Repeat once. Melt 423 g granulated sugar in a saucepan, add the blanched ginger and cook until 108°C. Roll the cooked ginger in castor sugar.

Filter Coffee Truffles

Dark chocolate paired with a light south Indian filter coffee flavour gives these truffles a wonderfully nutty taste. A vegan recipe, it's a healthier alternative to the other chocolates I've created.

MAKES 12 PIECES

INGREDIENTS
DECOCTION
South Indian coffee powder 110 g

GANACHE
Filter coffee powder (ground fine) 110 g
Decoction 140 ml
Dark chocolate 140 g

COATING
Dark chocolate 90 g
Cocoa powder 60 g

☀ To get that authentic south Indian coffee flavour, you will need a filter coffee percolator. Add the coffee powder in the upper chamber of the percolator and pack or tamp it. Fill boiling water till the maximum water line in the upper chamber and let the coffee brew and drip into the lower chamber. Preferably, leave it overnight.

☀ Melt the dark chocolate over a double boiler till smooth.

☀ Combine 140 ml coffee decoction and the ground coffee powder with the melted dark chocolate.

☀ Mix well and chill in the fridge for 30 to 40 minutes or till the ganache is pliable and can be rolled.

☀ Measure 15 g pieces of ganache, roll into balls and set on a baking sheet. Chill in the freezer for 15 to 20 minutes. (This ganache will be extremely wet since it contains a large amount of water, so it is important to freeze it so that the chocolate balls set properly.)

☀ For the coating, melt 90 g dark chocolate over a double boiler till smooth.

☀ Using a toothpick or skewer, dip the ganache balls into the melted chocolate and coat evenly. Tap to remove excess chocolate. Chill in the fridge till set. Before serving roll the truffles in cocoa powder. These truffles can be stored in the fridge for up to 3 days.

Use a south Indian coffee brand like Cothas. It's one of the most famous brands of south Indian coffee from Bengaluru and can be ordered online. I feel this brand gives the best flavour of south Indian coffee. I usually prefer a coffee with 20 per cent chicory but if you like a stronger flavour, you can add more (I wouldn't recommend going beyond 30 per cent).

Aamras Truffles

Aamras, or mango pulp, is a summery sweet treat best paired with hot puris. These vegan truffles offer the same luscious flavour without the additional calories.

MAKES 12 PIECES

INGREDIENTS
Mango puree 120 g
White chocolate bar
150 g
A pinch of dried ginger
powder (sonth)

COATING
White chocolate 100 g
A few drops of yellow
food colouring gel

❋ Chop the white chocolate and place in a bowl.

❋ In a heavy-bottomed saucepan, add the mango puree and cook till the quantity is reduced to less than half its original size. Add the sonth, then take the reduced puree off the heat.

❋ Pour the warm mango puree over the chocolate and stir to make a smooth ganache.

❋ Once cool, transfer the ganache into the fridge for an hour.

❋ Measure 15 g of ganache and roll into balls.

❋ Melt 100 g white chocolate and add the yellow food colouring gel. Add very little and build the colour till you get a mango yellow.

❋ Dip the ganache balls into the chocolate and coat evenly. Using the tips of your fingers, lightly tap the truffle to give it some texture.

❋ Transfer the truffles onto a baking sheet and then into the fridge till they set. These truffles can be stored in the fridge for up to 3 days.

This recipe works with other fruit purees as well, like pink guava, pears, apple, etc. Omit the sonth and play around with other spices. Pair apple with cinnamon, pink guava with black salt, and pear with star anise.

Mac

arons

Basic Macaron Shell

A macaron is a delicate sandwich cookie made with almond flour, egg whites and sugar. In this section, I've paired it with different types of meetha-inspired fillings. This is a basic macaron shell recipe that you can play around with.

MAKES 20 MACARONS

INGREDIENTS
Icing sugar 100 g
Almond powder 140 g
Egg white 92 g
Castor sugar 120 g
Water 40 ml

1. Preheat the oven to 130°C and line two trays with baking paper.

2. Combine the almond powder and icing sugar in a food processor and pulse to get a fine crumb. Pass it through a fine sieve into a large mixing bowl and set aside. If there are any large pieces remaining, pop them back into the food processor and grind.

3. Add 42 g egg whites to the almond mixture and mix thoroughly.

4. In another bowl, or the bowl of a stand mixer, beat 50 g egg whites into stiff peaks.

5. Combine the granulated sugar and water in a small, heavy-based saucepan and heat on medium-low to 118°C, without stirring. Take the sugar syrup off the heat.

6. Start the whisk on low speed (to avoid splashing hot syrup), and slowly add the cooked sugar syrup to the beaten egg whites. Whisk at high speed until the mixture is cool. The mixture should increase in volume and become a firm, shiny and thick meringue, and have a beak when you lift the whisk.

7. Fold the meringue into the almond mixture, squashing and folding the mixture while rotating the bowl a quarter of a turn with each fold. Mix until you have a homogenous batter that runs from the spatula in a thick ribbon.

8. Transfer the mixture into a piping bag fitted with a round tip.

9. Pipe equal sized discs, about 1 1/2 inches in diameter, onto the baking sheets. Tap the sheet firmly on the bench several times to release air bubbles and obtain a smooth surface. Leave the tray to rest at room temperature for at least 20 minutes until a slight skin forms.

10. Bake the macarons for 15 to 18 minutes. Take the tray out of the oven, remove the parchment paper with the shells still on it and place on a cooling rack for at least 30 minutes or until completely cool. Remove macaron shells carefully from the baking paper.

When making macarons, it is essential to make sure that the bowl used to whip the egg whites is squeaky clean. For stiff peaks, ensure there is no oil residue at all.

Test the baked macarons by giving the tops of the shells a gentle nudge. If the tops don't move away from the feet, the macarons are done. If they move, pop the sheet back into the oven for another minute or two, then test again. Remember, the macarons should not brown.

Kashmiri Kahwa Tea Macarons

I love how warm Kahwa tea, brimming with Kashmiri green tea leaves, whole spices, nuts and saffron, makes you feel, especially in winter. These macarons give you that same fuzzy feeling, no matter what the weather outside is.

MAKES 20 MACARONS

INGREDIENTS

SHELL
See Basic Macaron Shell recipe on pp. 98-99
A few drops of green food colouring gel

FILLING
Green tea 25 g
Water 250 ml
Saffron strands 10 to 12
Cinnamon 1 medium stick
Clove 1
Cardamom, split 1 pod
Dried rose petals 1/2 tsp
Almonds, chopped 10 g
White chocolate 270 g

GARNISH
White chocolate, melted 30 g
Pistachios, chopped 20 g

✳ Whip up the macaron shell with the icing sugar, almond powder, castor sugar, water and egg whites (See pp. 98-99 for recipe). When you reach Step 7, add green food colouring to get a pistachio green colour.

✳ For the filling, heat water in a pan.

✳ Add the saffron, cinnamon, clove, cardamom and rose petals and boil for four to five minutes or until the water reduces by half.

✳ Take the pan off the heat and add the green tea leaves and cover. Let the tea steep into the water for a few minutes. Strain and set aside.

✳ Melt the white chocolate over a double boiler and add the tea water to it. Add the chopped almonds.

✳ Chill in the fridge for 10 minutes or until it's a pipeable consistency.

✳ Transfer the ganache filling into a piping bag and fill the macarons.

✳ Fill another piping bag with melted white chocolate and pipe lines across the macarons. Garnish with chopped pistachios.

These macarons look beautiful when decorated with tiny sugar flowers which you can find in any baking store. See Maghai Paan Truffle recipe (pp. 82-83) for how to make crystalised flowers at home.

Coconut & Cardamom Macaron

This is a twist on a classic coconut cake, where the sharp taste of elaichi takes the mellow macaron flavour up by a notch. A delicious accompaniment to afternoon tea.

MAKES 20
MACARONS

INGREDIENTS
SHELL
See Basic Macaron Shell recipe on pp. 98-99
Desiccated coconut 60 g

FILLING
White chocolate 270 g
Heavy cream 54 g
Cardamom powder 1/2 tsp

* Whip up the macaron shell with the icing sugar, almond powder, castor sugar, water and egg whites (See pp. 98-99 for recipe). When you reach Step 9, sprinkle the shells with desiccated coconut.

* For the filling, roughly chop white chocolate and transfer to a clean bowl.

* In a heavy-bottomed saucepan, heat the cream and cardamom powder till it starts to simmer.

* Remove from the heat and pour over the white chocolate. Let it sit for a minute, then stir until smooth.

* Cool the ganache in the fridge until it's soft but pipeable.

* Transfer the ganache filling into a piping bag and fill the macarons.

Saffron Macarons

This macaron has a light, perfumed flavour of saffron that is both delicate and exquisite.

MAKES 20
MACARONS

INGREDIENTS
SHELL
See Basic Macaron Shell recipe on pp. 98-99
A few drops of yellow food colouring gel

FILLING
White chocolate 270 g
Heavy cream 54 g
Water 20 ml
A pinch of saffron strands

✳ Whip up the macaron shell with the icing sugar, almond powder, castor sugar, water and egg whites (See pp. 98-99 for recipe). When you reach Step 7, divide the mixture into two bowls and add yellow food colouring to one bowl. The mixture should be a light yellow colour. When you transfer the mixture to the piping bag in Step 8, fill one half with the plain mixture and the other with the yellow mixture.

✳ For the filling, warm 20 ml water and add the saffron. Set aside to steep.

✳ Roughly chop the white chocolate and set aside in a bowl.

✳ In a heavy-bottomed saucepan, bring the heavy cream to a boil. Pour the cream and saffron water over the white chocolate and let it stand for a minute. Stir till the ganache is smooth and glossy. The saffron will naturally colour the ganache.

✳ Transfer the filling into a piping bag and fill the macarons.

If the ganache is too wet to pipe into the shells, pop the piping bag into the fridge for a few minutes before filling.

Thandai Macarons

A chilled milk drink bursting with dry fruits and fragrant spices, thandai is synonymous with the festival of Holi. Decorating these macaron shells can be colourful fun!

MAKES 20
MACARONS

INGREDIENTS
SHELL
See Basic Macaron Shell recipe on pp. 98-99
Red Velvet cake crumbs 100 g

FILLING
Thandai 140 g
White chocolate 270 g
Heavy cream 20 g

GARNISH
Cocoa butter 50 g
A few drops of red food colouring gel

* Whip up the macaron shell with the icing sugar, almond powder, castor sugar, water and egg whites (See pp. 98-99 for recipe). When you reach Step 9, sprinkle the shells with red velvet crumbs.

* For the filling, heat the thandai in a saucepan and reduce it by almost half. Set aside.

* Roughly chop the white chocolate and transfer it to a clean bowl.

* In a heavy-bottomed saucepan, heat the cream and bring it to a simmer.

* Pour the warm cream over the chocolate. Let it sit for a minute before stirring until smooth.

* Add the thandai and mix to incorporate evenly.

* Cool the ganache in the fridge to thicken (it should be soft and able to hold its shape). Transfer the ganache filling into a piping bag and fill the macarons.

* For garnish, mix the cocoa butter and red colour till smooth. Using a brush, draw a single stroke of the mixture across the macron shells.

To create a splatter effect of multiple colours, dip a brush into each colour and tap from a height on the macaron shell. These look great for a Holi party.

Jim Jam Macarons

Britannia's Jim Jam biscuits have always been my favourite teatime snack, so I decided to give them a more sophisticated avataar with this recipe.

MAKES 20 MACARONS

INGREDIENTS

SHELL
See Basic Macaron Shell recipe on pp. 98-99
A few drops of red gel food colouring

FILLING
Unsalted butter, chilled 120 g
Icing sugar 120 g
Vanilla essence 4 to 5 drops
Raspberry jam 200 g

❋ Whip up the macaron shell with the icing sugar, almond powder, castor sugar, water and egg whites (See pp. 98-99 for recipe). When you reach Step 7, add the red food colouring.

❋ For the filling, beat the butter and icing sugar to a smooth buttercream.

❋ Transfer the buttercream into a piping bag fitted with a star nozzle. Pipe stars around the edges of the macarons, leaving the centre empty.

❋ Fill the centre with a dollop of raspberry jam and top with a macaron shell.

Use a tart, seedless raspberry jam like Bonne Maman or Hero. A very sugary preserve will give you an overly sweet macaron which you don't want.

Til Chikki Macarons

This is my light, airy interpretation of chikki. The tahini and honey intensify the sesame flavour, and the shell of the macarons adds that quintessential crunch.

MAKES 20 MACARONS

INGREDIENTS
SHELL
See Basic Macaron Shell recipe on pp. 98-99
A few drops of black food colouring gel
Black and white sesame seeds (til), toasted 1 tsp

FILLING
Honey 25 g
Tahini 34 g
Til chikki, ground 25 g
Black sesame seeds (til), toasted 50 g
Dark chocolate 175 g

* Whip up the macaron shell with the icing sugar, almond powder, castor sugar, water and egg whites (See pp. 98-99 for recipe). When you reach Step 7, add black food colouring to the batter until it become becomes a deep black colour. At Step 9 garnish the piped batter discs with toasted black and white sesame seeds.

* For the filling, pulse the toasted sesame seeds in a grinder till they acquire a coarse texture.

* In a saucepan, warm the honey and add the tahini, ground til chikki and ground sesame seeds, and stir.

* Melt the dark chocolate over a double boiler and add the honey and til chikki mixture to it.

* Chill in the fridge for 10 minutes or until the filling is a pipeable consistency. Transfer the ganache filling into a piping bag and fill the macarons.

Ice C

& S

reams,
Kulfis
orbets

Tools

Nothing beats homemade ice cream, and using an ice cream maker will give you a smoother treat. While it's best to follow the manufacturer's instructions, keep these tips in mind:

* If your ice cream maker comes with a freezer bowl, be sure to freeze this bowl for at least 24 hours before making ice cream. If the bowl is not cold enough, chances are your ice cream will never freeze.

* Turn on the motor before pouring the ice cream base into it. The bowl is so cold that the mixture will freeze immediately upon contact. With the machine in motion, you'll ensure the mixture doesn't become a frozen chunk in the bowl.

* Most machines take about 20 to 30 minutes to churn ice cream.

MAKING ICE CREAM MANUALLY

* If you don't have an ice cream machine, this is how you can manually churn your ice cream. Start by filling a large bowl about halfway with ice. Stir in 3/4 cup rock salt.

* Nestle a smaller bowl in the ice, burying it as much as possible. Fill the smaller bowl halfway with ice cream base (use at most 2 cups of mix).

* Using a hand mixer, beat the mix for 10 minutes. Partially cover the bowl with a towel to prevent spattering. The mix should get very cold to the touch, although it will probably not start transforming into actual ice cream.

* After you have beaten and chilled the mix for about 10 minutes, cover with a towel and place the entire set of nested bowls — large and small — in the freezer. Freeze for 45 minutes.

* Remove the bowls from the freezer. Draw a spoon across the top of the ice cream mix. It's probably the consistency of loose pudding, especially on top.

* Mix again with the hand mixer for 5 minutes. At this point the mixture should be the texture of soft-serve ice cream.

* Remove the small bowl from the large bowl, and cover the top with plastic wrap touching the surface of the ice cream. Freeze for an additional two hours, or overnight.

Rasmalai Ice Cream

I love rasmalai for its light, spongy texture, and because it's not overly sweet. This recipe is loaded with flavour, since I use both the pieces and the thick, creamy milk.

SERVES 15

INGREDIENTS
Kesar rasmalai milk
250 ml
Heavy cream 750 g
Castor sugar 200 g
Milk powder 100 g
Cornflour 12 g
Saffron 10 strands
Milk 100 ml
Kesar rasmalai 15 pcs

✳ In a heavy-bottomed saucepan, combine the rasmalai milk, cream, sugar, milk powder and saffron.

✳ Once the mixture comes to a boil, take it off the heat.

✳ In another saucepan, warm 100 ml of milk and pour it over the cornflour. Mix until smooth.

✳ Combine both mixtures in a saucepan and heat, stirring gently until the mixture coats the back of a wooden spoon. When you run your finger down the middle of the coated spoon, the mixture should hold its shape.

✳ Cool the mixture over an ice bath. Cover with plastic cling wrap and refrigerate overnight. Also, place the ice cream machine bowl in the freezer overnight.

✳ Churn the mixture on the following day in an ice cream machine till your ice cream thickens. If you don't have an ice cream machine, you can hand-churn till it sets (See pp. 114-115).

✳ Serve the ice cream with kesar rasmalai, either whole or cut into pieces.

You can go nuts (literally) garnishing this stunning ice cream. Use a combination of chopped nuts, saffron strands, silver varq and rose petals to create a visual and tasty treat.

Coconut Ice Cream with Imarti

This ice cream is my desi take on the Asian sticky honey noodles. You can also substitute the imarti, deep-fried spirals soaked in sugar syrup, with jalebis.

SERVES 6

INGREDIENTS
Coconut milk 250 ml
Cream 250 ml
Egg yolks 4
Castor sugar 125 g
Imarti 6 pieces

GARNISH
Black and white sesame seeds (til), toasted 1 tsp

* Heat the coconut milk and cream together and set aside.

* Make a sabayon (a light, mousse-like Italian dessert) by whisking the egg yolks and sugar over a double boiler until light and foamy.

* Take the sabayon off the double boiler, and add the coconut cream mixture to it. Combine well and strain.

* Cool the mixture over an ice bath. Cover with plastic cling wrap and refrigerate overnight. Also, place the ice cream machine bowl in the freezer overnight.

* Churn the mixture on the following day in an ice cream machine till your ice cream thickens. If you don't have an ice cream machine, you can hand-churn till it sets (See pp. 114-115).

* To serve, place a scoop of ice cream over each piece of imarti, and garnish with toasted sesame seeds.

Hand-churning ice cream can be daunting task, but this method works brilliantly. The secret is to constantly agitate the ice cream mixture to ensure a smooth, creamy consistency.

Chocolate Chilli Ice Cream

This ice cream, made with fiery Bird's eye chillies, packs a dangerous amount of spice, but the dark chocolate cuts through the heat. The kick of the chilli gives an unusual twist to this deliciously cold treat.

SERVES 15

INGREDIENTS
Milk 500 ml
Cream 60 g
Dark chocolate, chopped 210 g
Egg yolk 120 g
Castor sugar 180 g
Bird's eye chillies 5 pieces
Cocoa powder 50 g

* Deseed the chillies and chop finely.

* Blanch the chillies by immersing them in hot water and then in ice-cold water, to reduce the heat of the chiles.

* In a saucepan, heat the milk and cream till it reaches 60°C. Add the cocoa powder. Remove the pan from the stove.

* In a medium-sized bowl, whisk the egg yolks with sugar.

* Stir the egg yolk mixture into the milk and further cook it to 72°C. Then remove the mixture from the heat, and add the chillies.

* Strain the custard through a sieve and pour over the dark chocolate pieces. Let it rest for a few seconds before stirring till smooth.

* Cool the mixture over an ice bath. Cover with plastic cling wrap and refrigerate overnight. Also, place the ice cream machine bowl in the freezer overnight.

* Churn the mixture on the following day in an ice cream machine till your ice cream thickens. If you don't have an ice cream machine, you can hand-churn till it sets (See pp. 114-115).

Garnish the ice cream with either grated dark chocolate or a drizzle of melted chocolate sauce. If you can't find Bird's eye chillies, any fresh, red variety will work.

Rose Kulfi

The beauty of kulfi lies in its simplicity – it's basically milk, sugar and natural flavours. This is my Mum's recipe and it's a sweet favourite in our home.

SERVES 15

INGREDIENTS
Milk 350 ml
Cream 750 g
Castor sugar 200 g
Milk powder 100 g
Cornflour 12 g
Rose syrup 180 ml

GARNISH
Pistachio, chopped 60 g

✳ In a heavy-bottomed saucepan combine 250 ml milk, cream, castor sugar and milk powder.

✳ Bring all the ingredients to a boil and then remove the pan from heat.

✳ In another saucepan, warm 100 ml of milk and pour it over the cornflour. Mix well till you get a smooth paste.

✳ Combine both mixtures in a saucepan and heat, stirring gently until the mixture coats the back of a wooden spoon. When you run your finger down the middle of the coated spoon, the mixture should hold its shape.

✳ Take the mixture off the heat, add the rose syrup and mix well.

✳ Cool the mixture completely over an ice bath.

✳ Pour this mixture into kulfi moulds and set overnight in the freezer.

✳ To unmould the kulfi, dip the moulds in room temperature water and loosen the sides first.

✳ Garnish the kulfi with chopped pistachios.

You can garnish this kulfi with a variety of chopped nuts and dry fruits. Edible rose petals also look stunning over these popsicles.

Salted Caramel Kulfi

Just the right balance of salty and sweet, the rich,
decadent flavour of salted caramel is a crowd favourite.
With this kulfi, I've given it a desi twist.

SERVES 15

INGREDIENTS

Plain malai kulfi 1.2 kg
Castor sugar 390 g
Salted butter 40 g
Heavy cream 390 g
Liquid glucose 50 g

GARNISH

Maldon sea salt 1 tsp

* In a heavy-bottomed saucepan, heat liquid glucose and sugar on medium heat.

* Stir constantly till the sugar dissolves and mixture starts to gently bubble.

* Increase the heat, bring it to boil and stop stirring.

* Let mixture continue boiling until it turns amber in colour. This will take 8 to 10 minutes.

* Add butter to deglaze the pan.

* Remove from heat and slowly whisk in cream to make the salted caramel.

* Add the salt and mix well.

* Melt the store-bought kulfi in a bowl till it's liquid in consistency.

* Add the salted caramel and stir. Reserve some of the caramel for the garnish.

* Pour this mixture into kulfi moulds and set it overnight in the freezer. To unmould, dip the moulds in warm water to loosen the kulfi.

* Garnish with a sprinkle of sea salt and drizzle of salted caramel sauce.

Use a good quality kulfi, one with a high fat content which has a creamy consistency rather than an icy, grainy one. I love using Parsi Dairy Farm kulfi.

Guava Chilli Sorbet

Who doesn't have memories of munching on guava with chilli powder and salt? This tangy sorbet will take you back in time and is perfect for the hot summers.

SERVES 15

INGREDIENTS
Guava juice 1 l
Castor sugar 100 g
Liquid glucose 50 g
Bird's eye chillies 5 pieces
Black salt 1/2 tbsp
Chat masala 1 tsp
Crushed black pepper 1/2 tsp

❋ Deseed the Bird's eye chillies and chop finely.

❋ Blanch the chillies by immersing them in hot water and then ice-cold water. Repeat this twice to dull the spiciness of the chillies.

❋ In a saucepan, combine the guava juice, blanched chillies, sugar, liquid glucose, salt and crushed black pepper.

❋ Simmer the mixture for 5 to 6 minutes.

❋ Remove the saucepan from the heat and cool the mixture over an ice bath. Cover with plastic cling wrap and refrigerate overnight. Also, place the ice cream machine bowl in the freezer overnight.

❋ Churn the mixture on the following day in an ice cream machine till your sorbet sets. If you don't have an ice cream machine, you can hand-churn till it sets (See pp. 114-115).

I prefer using pink guava juice for this recipe and I usually make fresh juice with pink guavas when in season. This recipe also works well with passion fruit.

Kopra Pak Ice Cream

Not just your typical coconut ice cream, this creamy concoction is packed with the intense flavour of kopra pak, a mithai made from coconut, sugar, milk and khoya.

SERVES 10

INGREDIENTS
White kopra pak 300 g
Milk 350 ml
Heavy cream 750 g
Castor sugar 160 g
Coconut milk powder
100 g
Cornflour 1.3 tbsp

GARNISH
Pieces of kopra pak

※ In a heavy-bottomed saucepan combine 250 ml milk, cream, sugar and coconut milk powder.

※ Once the mixture reaches a boil, remove it from the heat.

※ In another saucepan, warm 100 ml of milk and pour it over the cornflour. Mix well till it becomes a smooth paste.

※ Combine both mixtures into one saucepan and heat, stirring gently until the mixture coats the back of a wooden spoon. When you run your finger down the middle of the coated spoon, the mixture should hold its shape.

※ Cool the mixture over an ice bath. Cover with plastic cling wrap and refrigerate overnight. Also, place the ice cream machine bowl in the freezer overnight.

※ On the following day, add broken bits of kopra pak to the mixture. Then churn in an ice cream machine till your ice cream thickens. If you don't have an ice cream machine, you can hand-churn till it sets (See pp. 114-115).

※ Garnish with pieces of kopra pak.

If you prefer your ice cream smooth, omit the kopra pak in the mixture and just use 100 g as garnish. Your ice cream will still have a luscious, coconutty flavour.

Kala Khatta Sorbet

I have fond memories of kala khatta chuskis that would stain my tongue a vibrant purple. This sorbet is my tribute to that childhood memory.

SERVES 15

INGREDIENTS
Water 500 ml
Kala khatta syrup
500 ml
Castor sugar 40 g
Liquid glucose 100 g
Black salt 1 tsp
Black pepper powder
1/4 tsp
Lemon juice 20 ml

GARNISH
Chaat masala to taste

✻ In a saucepan, combine water with liquid glucose and sugar. Bring the mixture to a boil, then remove the saucepan from the heat and allow it to cool completely.

✻ Add the kala khatta syrup, lemon juice, black pepper and black salt and mix well.

✻ Remove the saucepan from the heat and cool the mixture over an ice bath. Cover with plastic cling wrap and refrigerate overnight. Also, place the ice cream machine bowl in the freezer overnight.

✻ Churn the mixture on the following day in an ice cream machine till your sorbet sets. If you don't have an ice cream machine, you can hand-churn till it sets (See pp. 114-115).

✻ Serve once the sorbet is firm, with a pinch of chaat masala.

The sorbet tastes delicious when served with pomegranate seeds and mulberries. This recipe also works well as a granita (frozen fruit dessert). Instead of pulsing the sorbet after the first freeze, simply scrape it with a spoon and drizzle some kala khatta syrup on top.

Kitchen Conversions

LIQUID

Cups	Millilitres
1/4	60 ml
1/3	80 ml
1/2	120 ml
2/3	160 ml
3/4	180 ml
1	240 ml
2	475 ml
4	1 l

SOLID

Spoon	Grams	Millilitres
1/4 tsp	1 g	1 ml
1/2 tsp	2 g	2 ml
1 tsp	4 g	5 ml
1/2 tbsp	7 g	7.5 ml
1 tbsp	14.3 g	15 ml

BUTTER

Cups	Grams
1/4	57 g
1/4	76 g
1/2	113 g
1	227 g

SUGAR (GRANULATED)

Cups	Grams	Ounces
1/4	50 g	1.78 oz
1/3	67 g	2.37 oz
1/2	100 g	3.55 oz
2/3	134 g	4.73 oz
3/4	150 g	5.3 oz
1	201 g	7.1 oz

FLOUR/CONFECTIONER'S SUGAR/CHOCOLATE POWDER

Cups	Grams	Ounces
1/4	32 g	1.13 oz
1/3	43 g	1.5 oz
1/2	64 g	2.25 oz
2/3	85 g	3 oz
3/4	96 g	3.38 oz
1	128 g	4.5 oz

CHOCOLATE CHIPS

Cup	Grams	Ounces
1/4	45 g	1.5 oz
1/3	60 g	2.1 oz
1/2	90 g	3.1 oz
2/3	115 g	4.1 oz
3/4	130 g	4.6 oz
1	175 g	6.2 oz
2	350 g	12.3 oz

OVEN TEMPERATURE

Fahrenheit	Celcius
250	120
300	150
325	170
350	180
375	190
400	200
425	220

Index

ACKNOWLEDGEMENTS

A huge thank you to Ananth Padmanabhan, Sonal Nerurkar, Bonita Vaz Shimray and the wonderful team at HarperCollins India for putting this book together. Thank you to Prateeksh Mehra and Shreya Gupta for beautifully capturing the images in the book, and for executing my vision perfectly.

A big thank you to Joseph Radhik for shooting the fabulous cover and for always being there to capture the important moments in my life.

Thank you to my entire team at our central kitchen, Chef Amit Bhatia and Chef Nilesh Mandadkar for their tireless dedication to this book, and for allowing me to turn our central kitchen into a creative playground.

Most importantly, thank you to my wonderful family. My Dad, Viveck Goenka, for a continuous supply of sound advice; my Mum, Zita Goenka, for encouraging me to always dream bigger; and my sister, Sasha Goenka, my sous chef in life.

Thank you to the second most amazing man on this planet (the first being our son), my best friend and husband, Karan Khetarpal. The reason I fell in love with food was you and the reason I believe in love is you.

Last, but not least, thank you to my son, Kabir. You make me want to be the best version of myself every single day.

First published in India by
HarperCollins *Publishers* in 2019
A-75, Sector 57, Noida, Uttar Pradesh 201301, India
www.harpercollins.co.in

P-ISBN 978-93-5357-360-7
E-ISBN – 978-93-5357-361-4

Designed by HarperCollins *Publishers* India
Printed and bound at Thomson Press (India) Ltd
Cover Photo **Joseph Radhik**
Photography **Prateeksh Mehra**
Styling **Shreya Gupta**
Design **Divya Saxena**